Daybreak on the Water

Gary Lark

Flowstone Press

Daybreak on the Water
Copyright © 2020 Gary Lark

Cover photo "Watercourse"
by David Lorenz Winston
used with permission

Flowstone Press,
an Imprint of Left Fork
www.leftfork.org/flowstone

First Flowstone Press Edition • September 2020
ISBN 978-1-945824-39-5

Daybreak on the Water

"I am haunted by waters."

— Norman Maclean,
A River Runs Through It

Province of Dragonflies

Golden Mean	3
Rock Creek Camp	4
Copeland Creek	7
Wells Creek Run	8
The Sheriff Works Sundays	10
Phantom	11
After Work	13
Yellow Boat	14
Chinook	16
Will and Luck	18
Sonny	20
Industry	22
The Meal	23
Water Worn	24
Corn and Steelhead	25
Road to Heaven	27
First Cast	28
River Bend	29
Daybreak, Eagle Rock	30
Wading	31

In Stream

Flying Lesson	35
In Stream	37
Monsters All	39
Protocol	40
Lost	41
Wilderness	42
Around the Bend	44
Brockton Store	45
Clams	48
Winter	50
Steamboat Don	51
Return	53
Long Way Home	54
Crucible	55
Nowhere	56
Osprey	57
Last Time	58
Stone	59
Cable Crossing	60

Province of Dragonflies

Golden Mean

To be
at once the mountain
the valley
and the trout
that swims between.

Rock Creek Camp

I

In the gray morning
down the slip-slop
muddy trails of winter
ragged children in hand-made
hand-me-down clothes
straggle toward the school bus
like raindrops down
a rumpled face.

Tar-paper, board and shingle
shacks perch on pole legs
like birds with opal eyes,
the logging camp halfway
between the cut
and the echo.

On countless mornings
men crawl into a crummy
and head for the show—
to fall, buck and load
the receding timber.
Donkey engines and high leads
winch giant Douglas fir
to the landing
where trucks line up
ready to roll down the mountain.
At a cold sunrise
the whip of the choker cable
can whisper your name.

Women hang the wash
by the wood stove
with a baby on one hip,
make a yeast sponge
and let the bread rise,
wish the radio signal
came in during the day.
The portable Singer
rests on the kitchen table
halfway through a shirt.

      II
Among the scents
of pine and fir and moss,
musk of decay,
chanterelles, hedgehogs and morels
push up through beetle dung and elk scat.
Huckleberry and hemlock
grow from the sloughing cells
of a giant cedar laid down
after centuries of life,
new green reaching for the light.

For children, wild in the long round summer,
there's trout and thimble berries,
a rope you take up the cottonwood
as high as you dare
then swing out and out
and fly into the clear cold water,
hunt your dreams through
the thickets of alder,
lay in the sweet summer grass
lost in the meadow.

III
Loaded log trucks
snake their way
out of the foothills.
There will come a day
when the children walk
out of the hills
and the adults move to the city.
Camps and mill towns evaporate
as money pools are drained
leaving a few weathered boards
rotting in the moss.

Copeland Creek

Long before they were paved, we drove
the stutter of washboard roads,
pounded endlessly by log trucks,
thirty miles up Adam's bony ribs
to a paradise called Copeland Creek.

We camped where the creek spills
into the North Umpqua.
I was eight years old
and the river sang.

After sleeping in the river's voice,
my father, his friend, and I
put fly rods together,
mine a nine foot bamboo
with mended tip and casting reel
full of fly line.

We waded pool to pool,
side to side, the flash of silver
filling our creels.
There were pools too deep,
so the closest man would grab
my free hand and pull me,
half swimming,
to the next gravel bar.

Back at camp, morning light
still filtering through fir needles,
mother tended Dutch oven biscuits
as trout curled in the frying pan.
There's a part of me still there
surrounded by enormous trees
the river singing me alive.

Wells Creek Run

Dawn not yet come,
we're in father's work truck
making for the lower river.
He smells of coffee and tobacco
though he's not smoking,
the heater pumping on our feet.
A muzzy light starts in the trees
and the river comes to us
curling around the hills
as if there was nothing
before the living water
and the trout upon its wet nerve.

Over half way there
we meet Sonny at Arlene's Café.
There's steam and smoke,
loggers and fishermen,
clouds of conversation,
our feet on straight-grain fir
cut from the first hundred feet
of a three hundred year old tree
fifty years ago.
I feel the spring in the oiled planks
when we walk to a table
and order sausage, eggs and potatoes.

We pull up at the Wells Creek bridge
and wrestle the aluminum boat
from the top of Sonny's station wagon,
we slide it down the creek spill
to the glass face of river.
Motor and tackle and then we're moving
out into a mirror of maple trees
and grass, and the sleeping house

on the far side. I wonder about it,
not seeing a road or bridge
or even a boat. Maybe it sprouted there
like a mushroom.

The troll wake-lines disappear
among the rocks and shadows.
Sonny smokes Chesterfields
and fidgets, checking his line,
running the motor and talking
about fishing the bay down river
when he was young.
The sun comes through a gap ahead of us.

The chug-purr of the Evinrude,
the bobbing rhythm of spinners,
the suspended life before,
the dangling life after,
we are held in a separate universe,
this river air.

The Sheriff Works Sundays

We're swimming on a Sunday afternoon
where the placid water makes for the bend
when we hear a boat coming fast up river
(fast in those days was a 25 horse at full throttle)
with Jimmy Cottrell and Sven Hardesty
ducked down to decrease their wind resistance
and looking guilty of some sin
we want to know about.
They whizz by, the sheriff's sled boat
hard behind them. My brother says,
"Come on, let's go."
I didn't think we had a chance,
but I'm right behind him
putting on my britches and running
like the devil between river cottonwoods
and the hay field, then up through Vann's carrots
and the apple orchard, almost to the rapids
above the stone-set spikes used to attach gillnets
a generation ago and maple trees hanging out over the water
where I hooked a Coho in the smooth green mirror last fall.
There they are with the sheriff
towing their boat and them in handcuffs.
My brother says, "There's a deer in there."
Sure enough, I can see its tan side lying
in the front of the boat.
It's a little anticlimactic, it being a deer
jacked out of season.
Venison is eaten year round in this valley
but it's a public shame to get caught.
Our swimming time wasted,
we go back up to the house
to see if there's any watermelon left.

Phantom

It was spring going into summer,
after a brief storm, the river up
a bit and milky,
but I was throwing a spinner anyway,
along the main current
and around willow tufted islands
when I snagged a rock.
I tugged upstream and down.
Gave it slack, hoping the pull of current
would dislodge the hook.
I broke the line with no replacement.
Used flies adorned my red felt hat.
I tied one on the eight pound line
of the spinning rod, an outfit
designed not to work in the best of conditions.

As I hopped rock to rock, wading,
I dabbling a Coachman behind an island,
a phantom of the deep rose,
grabbed the fly, then ran into the current.
My first encounter with a steelhead,
a yard long and determined.
It ran to the other side of a rock ledge.
A rock wall between it and me.
It ran down and back up
but stayed behind the ledge
sawing on the line.

Water, the freshened air, bright sky,
poison oak and greasewood thickets
running up the bluff behind me.
On the top sat the country club
with its dining room and bar
looking out into the distance,

a place I'd never be,
a place my father made fun of with his nose in the air
saying he could find a cheaper place to get drunk
and swap his wife, for which my mother
would give him a knock.
People in the dining room looked out
but couldn't see down where I tugged on the line.

There was a lower spot on the rock,
relatively smooth and when the fish was near
I pulled until it was on the rock
and I gave it one more tug.
The line broke.
The steelhead gave a flip
and sank out of sight.
It was there
and then it wasn't.

After Work

He would come home with the shape
of welding goggles impressed around his eyes.
We would throw our fly rods
in the back of the truck
and head up Little River
with a foot of daylight
hanging in the west.
Not much was said on the way.
An early June day sliding beneath us,
the water singing, father upstream
and me down, jumping, wading,
fishing the channels,
it was all we needed.

Yellow Boat

The skeletons were pieced together
in Dale's backyard.
Twin boats, modified V bottom,
Chris Craft pattern,
built on weekends or after work,
thin plywood on fir ribs
and oak strips steamed in irrigation pipe
fit to a mold for the keel or gunnels,
fiberglass laid over the plywood,
painted and painted again.
Yellow and black.
Not one of those runabouts
you see in the movies,
these were fishing boats,
good ones for the river or bay.

It sat in the water at the end of the road,
outboard and gear left spring, summer
and into the fall. That's the way it was,
and no one ever lost so much as a sinker.
We fished, hunted ducks and cruised
the water below the forks for ten years
in the only by-god-lemon-yellow boat
on the entire Umpqua river system.

Wooden boats were green
and a few blue. When the fiberglass
and plastic came in there were white
and red but it would take years
before I saw another yellow boat
and it was towing skiers.

Years later I pondered why
my mild mannered father chose yellow.

My mother cleared it up:
when they were dancing
to swing music in 1938
my father had a golden sash
sewn in his bell bottoms
that would flash on every turn.

Chinook

It was between summer steelhead
and early fall chinook,
before the family moved upriver
and my brother disappeared into the Air Force.
Our farm was to be sold
and stilled heat lay in the fields.
We were fishing anyway.
Late summer, early fall,
a place as divine as I would ever know,
the river placid and clear
with ash leaves turning,
gray squirrels rustling for myrtle nuts.
My brother always preferred trolling
this slack water for days if necessary
to catch that one big fish.
I was more impatient. I liked
the smaller streams, wading cold water,
flipping a fly into the shadows
for a pan full of trout.
But here we are, motor purring,
and wham, Leon's rod bends double.
It's a monster. His excitement contagious.
A dorsal fin cuts the water, running hard,
then it sounds, holding in a deep spot.
I cut the motor, pull it up out of the way.
It didn't jump like a steelhead,
those wild sea-run trout,
but twisted and roiled in the current
pulling us down river.
We let it, the next rapids not a worry.
Leon would get it near the boat
and it would dive away.
When it was close and tired
I slipped the net under the mottled silver body.

It was too big for me to lift.
Boat leaning, Leon grabbed the net
and we hoisted the chinook onboard.
It was a beauty, the largest fish
either of us would ever catch.
He didn't let it get away.
We drove to town, the forty-five pound fish
lying on the floor in front of the back seat
of the green 1947 Chevy
our grandfather had given Leon
when he quit driving.
We drove by the office where mom worked.
We drove by to show a high school friend.
When there was no one else
and there was fear of spoiled fish
we went home and cut it up for the freezer.
We would fish a few more times
before the world took us into other currents
but that day would never be repeated.

Will and Luck

We camped at Crystal Springs
where bright clear water gurgled
from the ground and ran to the reservoir
The mosquitoes weren't too bad.
Father was back home working
14 hour days refurbishing the mill.
His crew worked while everybody else
took vacation. Happened every year.
So my brother, mother and I
packed away for a couple days
in the high country.

The first afternoon, when shadows
were right, we took the flume road
down the canyon and slid a steep side
to the stream below the dam.
My brother went upstream and I down.
The fly dropped into the water
and three fish rushed for it.
I had my limit of ten in half an hour
and went to check on my brother.
He had eight. Eighteen was enough
for dinner so we started looking
for a way up, out of the canyon.

Sliding into the canyon had its hazards
but climbing out was a special case.
It wasn't too hard to angle up
but that few yards over the lip
near the road took will and luck.
I'd get within arm's reach
and the dust and gravel bulged.
That's where the will came in,
I would half throw myself,

fly rod and creel full of fish
over that last incline.
It worked on the first try
most of the time.

Back at camp the guy in the next camp over
couldn't help seeing us frying fish.
People bank fished or trolled
the reservoir in small boats,
now and then catching a lunker brown
but most caught the bottom.
"Where'd you catch those," he asked.
"Down a ways," we answered.
We were vague and he knew it,
but fisherman's code let it die right there.
We had a couple dinners of trout,
gloating only a little.

A few years later I went back to the canyon
and found fewer fish and more footprints.
There aren't many places left
where you drop in a fly and fish run at it.
I found a place in the Wallowas,
a mile down from a road crossing
and a short hike through the trees,
where the trout are undisturbed.
But that's all I'm saying.

Sonny

I've known a few fishing fools
but Sonny tips the scales.
At one time he owned half a music store:
musical instruments, pianos,
sheet music, stands and mutes,
and TVs when they first came out.

We used to go to Sonny's house
for a weekly American communion
with Disney and Lawrence Welk.
His daughter and I were friends
running wild by the river,
picking Oregon tea and licorice fern.
Rumor had it he was master of the fiddle,
had played far and wide as a young man
but by this time he'd put it away for good.

Sonny had an eighteen foot flat bottom river boat
down by his in-law's house for every fish run.
We camped together at Copeland Creek
eating pans full of fat little mountain trout.
Early spring he fished Elk and Hubbard Creeks.
We ran the main Umpqua from Sawyer Rapids
to the forks with his aluminum car topper.
He made the best smoked salmon I ever tasted.
Then he sold the store.

He rigged his river boat for long lining
and fished for salmon in the ocean.
We all thought he would drown,
pulling in fish between swells,
salmon piling around his feet
in a boat made for plowing soft river water.

The next year he had a seaworthy craft
and lived half the year near the boat basin.
In the dead of winter he was back on the river
trolling for winter steelhead, chugging
between the forks and the North Fork Bridge.
In the steady rain before flood water
lapped up the bank at the in-laws
he'd sink his eighteen footer in the muddy bottom
and wait for the river to drop.

All his stories had a piece of river in them.
Last time I saw Sonny the creases around his eyes
were cut deep by the sea wind.
There was only one home for him,
in a boat, on the water, checking his line.

Industry

Crystal was about forty-five
when she started to make those crazy things.
Lived across the pasture from us on a little hill.
She'd always been good with a sewing machine,
clothes for her kids, pillows, shawls,
little cloth boxes for Christmas.
But then these strange, odd, peculiar things
started to show up at the county fair:
dogs with alligator heads, snakes
with human heads and belled tails,
a turquoise starfish with a moon face,
four lifelike kittens on a sofa cushion.
A store owner uptown bought a few
and put them in his window.
One of his drummers took a couple
to a show in Denver.
In three years' time she had half a dozen neighbors
sewing for her in a converted barn.
The following year her husband Bob
leased out his pasture and hay field.
We started to see Bob down at the river
in a new boat. We'd anchor by him at the forks
and shoot the breeze, the warm sun
washing over us.

The Meal

Spirit made me flesh
in this river walking land
among the deer dance people,
singing the dreams awake.

Flesh made me spirit
in this dream of bone and water
to slip this thin skin
and walk between.

The platter is passed
from hand to hand
each tongue tasting the river
in the salmon's flesh.

Water Worn

Bill and I are upriver from Pete's house
fishing the slick above a rapids
before it bends at the bluff
and heads toward town.
Bill hooks a steelhead
about two-thirds the way across.
It does a tail dance
then heads downstream
on the other side of some rocks.
Bill's line gets hung up.
So I strip off and swim out
above the problem,
angling with the current
to hit the rock, lift the line
and go left of the rock
while the fish runs ahead of me.
It works like a charm
except the fish throws the hook.
I kick my feet up in front
and float through the channel
with a few water worn bumps
hitting my butt on the way.
There are some spots I wouldn't do this
but I've slid through this kind of water before,
just for fun, and you have to look out
for the rocks just below the surface
that bulge the water with a point.

Corn and Steelhead

Finley, our neighbor,
says let's fish the channels
and he, my father and I
go upriver to where bedrock
is exposed in the dead of summer
and the river is channeled between,
up to where the bridge crosses
and the bus I ride all school year
stops to pick up Ginger.
She's the highlight of the bus trip.
Ginger wouldn't give me the time of day
but I like looking at her anyway.

Finley and father head to the other side
where you can get to more channels
but there's a spot I've been watching
from the bus where a fir tree has fallen,
reaching out into the water on this side.
Finley likes to use night crawlers
threaded on the hook
and a piece of canned corn on the tip.
Never understood why.
The fish like worms just fine
without a vegetable.
Might as well throw in barbequed chicken
and a roll.

I've got a weighted yellow spinner
I've been using all summer
and from a space in the branches
of the fallen tree I fling it down river

and retrieve. Next cast up,
wham! a fish hits and runs
to the middle of the river.
After a few minutes I coax it in
through the fir needles
and there is another fish trailing it.
Father and Finley had barely arrived
on the other side when I hold up the fish
for them to see. The second fish
follows the lure another time
but won't grab it, so I try another.
Same result. I must report that
Finley and my father are skunked.

Summer steelhead, three to eight pounds,
are jewels in the bright water,
always a privilege to catch.
Next winter, flood water took the tree.
I had hoped to try it again.

Road to Heaven

The road to heaven
started somewhere near
Julie's backdoor.
That's where the glow began.
We walked the river path
through ferns, maples
and spring wild flowers
to the rocks and warm sand
benched in from winter's flood
with ripple marks
and little puzzles of driftwood.
The dazzle of the sunlit waves
pulled us in and in and in.
I was always amazed
that we were the only ones
burning.

First Cast

The lake, a glittering sky.
Fish dimple the clouds.
Reeds brush a mountain's cheek.
Morning canoe angles me through trees.
I ready my line and cast
in the province of dragonflies.

River Bend

There was sand grit under my feet,
water slipping by, a buzzard circling
the season of dying fish,
carcasses sprawled on washed stone.
They had spawned in home gravel
upstream, their redds older
than tree rings could tell.
I was still swimming upstream then
vigorous and dumb
the urge-on-urge pushing.
Now, the water still flows,
looks exactly the same.
It's flesh that crumbles.

Daybreak, Eagle Rock

Morning arrives
with a cool whisper.
River slides from mountain belly
lucent and green.

I flip a fly into the current,
strip out line that curls
between rush water
and boiling eddy.

A steelhead rises in the dream
we share, rumors my shadow
and fins to the chert bed,
sun rising for us all.

The scent of river mixes
with fir, pine and moss
as I set off down the trail.
The *creee* of osprey turns above.

Wading

When I'm thigh deep
the mood of water
moves me
like wind holds and challenges
a bird.

It's no weak wandering.
It carries the trial of mountains,
the life and death of unnumbered creatures.
Fish and crawdads, snakes and snails,
the wonderment of living things
whispered in the mud and sand,
in rock crevice and root.

I am in it,
of it.

In Stream

Flying Lesson

I was nineteen that summer,
working swing shift at the hospital,
running rivers with an old fiberglass boat,
velvet mornings to squander.
I don't remember deciding to fly
but one August morning
I stepped into a Cessna 150.
The instructor and owner of the place
gave me my first ride.
We cruised the hills and rivers,
did some touch-and-goes,
then followed the wind over Garden Valley.
He put us in a side stall
sliding sideways toward the ground.
"That's what happens when you don't have enough lift," he said.

He gave it full throttle
and pointed the nose at the sun
until the plane wouldn't climb anymore.
Vertical, we slid tail first toward the fields below.
I'm holding onto the wheel like a lifeline.
"Let go," he said.
A pause.
"You have to trust the airplane."
Not to hold on as you are falling defies instinct
but I followed his lead
and the plane dropped forward,
a little sideways,
then leveled.
Orchards and alfalfa,
the familiar river curling its way.

I would solo, circle high meadows
looking for elk and patterns
in the bear grass and lupine.

One summer day I followed the river
from where I learned to swim
up the smooth water to the forks,
the winch and tracks of the old boat launch
hidden in growth and flood debris,
over where I caught my first steelhead
and the place our family almost lived,
past the small dam with its fish counter,
on up to the loop of river where I spent five years
catching trout for lunch, panning gold
that never showed, and there was Mike
out in his yard, so I waggled my wings
and he waved. I'll always choose to believe
that he knew it was me.
We had built a smoke house together.
The first batch or two tasted like leather
hung in a chimney. My father
said we might brine them first.
So we layered them in salt and brown sugar
and the fish became palatable.

I cruised over my old high school,
up to the beginning of fly water
and turned out over the hills
where Bill's family sheep ranch
nestled on a creek, and Dennis'
place lay on the other side of the ridge.
Dennis now gone to the Coast Guard.
Up past Allen and Jerry's places,
their trombone and clarinet still
resounding from our Dixieland band.
Back over town to touch down
for the last time.
I would join Bill at university
letting my life drop forward
and a little sideways.

In Stream

It was a beautiful in-between.
The sky hanging bright from here to forever
where Don and I anchored, the north fork
lapping its music against the hull.
It was a long moment, a pause,
a bubble in space-time.
I was back from the cattle call induction center
where a young doctor classified me as 1Y
and sent me home. The Vietnam War
raged over the horizon, having already taken
classmates, and here I was cradled
on the buoyance of this stream
and the reprieve I knew to be vulnerable.
But here in the golden eye of summer,
isolated from the currents on shore,
I fished with almost complete freedom.

I worked at a VA hospital
with veterans from WWI, WWII and Korea.
I knew the hunted, haunted and broken,
all the variations on disturbed brains,
wards of men living a slow dying
locked in rooms and hallways
beyond any known help.
We took care of their daily needs,
kept them safe and fed.
A few would arise from catatonic stillness
and go home to the barrage of the world,
then come back in a few months.
In a year I would join the Army National Guard,
in two I would be in Fort Lewis
running the courses ground smooth
by thousands of other feet.

Water slapped the fiberglass hull,
nothing on the line but a spinner
and the pull of the current.

Monsters All

I'm fishing around little grass-tufted islands,
land a couple, keep one, when I haul in
a ten-inch rainbow. Taking out the hook
I see a little head down its gullet.
This greedy fish hadn't digested one meal
before going after the artificial bug I offered.
Heron and egret, otter and merganser,
kingfisher trying to swallow
a fish the size of its head, and me,
a bunch of marauders on this dappled stream.
I slit it open, feed guts and half swallowed fish
to the crawdads. Up at the house
I fry it for lunch.

Protocol

I'm fishing below the dam
when I hear the first boom.

Some good old boy from town
has a new shotgun
and is blasting the countryside.

When I come up from the river
I say a polite hello
and get the hell out of there.

Lost

It was somewhere between
dusk and dark
on a road off another road
when I saw a blur
coming full tilt
up along the river,
growing into a deer.
I thought it was going to run right into us
but it leaped
in one graceful arc
and was gone.
I couldn't see it was a buck
until it was fifteen feet away
where it gathered its power
to clear the car.
We had stopped
to figure out where we were,
headlights still on,
door cracked
for the dome light
on our map,
a soft cottonwood smell
filling the night.
I looked up
to see where the color changes
from side hair to belly hair,
the fine texture
forming runs and swirls
and legs passing over.

Wilderness

The Tyee campground was near empty
when we pulled in, late afternoon,
starting to feel hungry.
Got the tent up and went for a swim.
The mid-summer river luxuriously warm,
exposed bedrock water-carved,
the air a caress.
Then the camp stove and scrambled eggs
with crookneck squash
from a stand twelve miles back.

After exploring curves and pools
we watch an osprey hunt,
otters on the other side slide and flip
as they keep an eye on us.
A truck pulls into the space near our tent.
"It's not my fault you're so fuckin' dumb,"
comes through the leaves.
In insolent silence two men
and a woman set up camp.
There's a tamped down rage among them.
The woman's voice, in authority,
"You could have taken care of the freezers,
but no, you just let them go."
One of the men muttering.
"How was I to know?"
They plop down at the picnic table,
pouring whiskey into cups.

Should we pull up camp?
We walk down the road,
the campsites are full now.
We decide to stay the night
hoping they pass out sooner

than later. But they don't.
At nightfall we crawl into the tent,
light our candle lamp
and try to read.
It goes on, drunk and dismal.
They're not loud, just persistent.
They all work in the kitchen
of some resort upriver,
cook, assistant cook
and bottle washer,
holding grudges, keeping score,
for this infinite hell.
Unlike a bachelor party
they never get to the "I love you guys" stage.
Each has a role testifying
to the others' part in the drama.
Somewhere after midnight they go silent.

Morning, we're pulling tent stakes
and packing gear as they head to the river
fishing poles, bait and buckets in hand.
They are going fishing together.
Stuff stowed we decide on breakfast
somewhere down the road.

Around the Bend

We fished the south fork
for bullhead catfish
or steelhead in the winter
but seldom for trout.
I decided it was time to explore.
June, before it got too warm,
I headed upstream,
looking for water on BLM
or Forest Service land,
somewhere not posted.
On the map Cow Creek
makes a big loop
before joining the river.
I walk railroad ties
away from civilization,
catch a couple of trout,
nothing to get excited about,
when a sweet aroma
filters through the trees.
I follow, find some tiger lilies.
Though perfect in their own right,
it's not them.
Down more ties, around a bend,
the scent invades me,
tunnels into my cells.
There it is, wild azalea
in full bloom, filling the world
with its heavenly essence.
In the pantheon of aromas,
it could shoulder aside
gardenia and honeysuckle.
Wild azalea, unmatched.

Brockton Store

It was an old place
built to supply farmsteads
and logging families
when horses did the work.
A false front gave majesty
to the town that never sprang
up around it.

Dewey and I would steal
empty pop bottles off the back porch
come around front
and trade them in for full ones.
We'd sit in the summer grass
on the hill in back
and fish the sky for great ideas.

By about age ten
I had outgrown thievery
and settled for stories.
Oiled wood planks led
through a forest of canned goods,
bread loaves and dog food
to a large desk and a woodstove.
A fly-tying vice, always in use,
was surrounded by capes of feathers,
hooks and chenille.
Spinner blades, wire and jars of beads
were racked on the near wall.
Fishing poles and hunting rifles
lined the opposite wall.

I spent all spare winter hours
in one of the stove-side chairs
listening.

When the air seemed to dry up
I would prompt "Did you ever catch a sturgeon?"
Or, "How far west do antelope come?"

And Ernie from Western Auto,
a mile down the road,
would put his sandwich down
and tell about the old days
when they would fish for sturgeon
with giant hooks baited with beef liver
on clothesline cord. How their tails
would drag in the dirt hanging
from an eight-foot wagon bed
that was five feet from the ground.
And Bill, who didn't seem to work anywhere,
would say that antelope used to come
right up to the timber but mostly stayed
in sagebrush country
where they could see predators
a long way off.
And Nels would start stalking
a smart old buck through the manzanita
up on the south side of Spencer mountain.
By high school I had a few stories of my own.

It was somewhere in this time I noticed
a new crop of young thieves
setting empty bottles on the front counter
and getting a Nehi or Hires or Coke
the way I used to. I asked,
"You know where they're getting those bottles?"
"Oh, yeah, it's an old game."
"But you're losing money."
And he said, "When that breaks me,
then I guess I'll be broke."
That was all he said.

I drive by the empty shell
on a spring day when the grass
grows lush and bright green
running up to the sheep pasture
where huge oaks stand as before.
Paint peels. Unseen timbers rot.
No empty bottles on the back porch.
It's a pity, I think, speeding down the asphalt,
that no one is getting an education
there anymore.

Clams

Smith River morning.
Moon pulling the tide out
and we rush in, hauling shovels
and buckets across a trestle
to the island, mud skirts
bare of the wash.

Trains run to the sawmills
and paper mills to the south,
but when? We hurry
in our muck boots,
buckets banging our knees,
water and mud flashing
through the ties.

Luck is with us.
We climb down to the mud,
the seething edge of life
where clams suck the living wet world
down their siphons and grow fat.
These aren't your pretty razor clams,
no, these are soft shells, commoners
in fifteen inches of mud.
The limit is a generous thirty-six.

There are siphon holes everywhere
and Don opens one pit as I open another
exposing an almost continuous bed.
Clam after clam into the buckets.
Scoop a little bay water in
before it gets too heavy.
Add more clams.
"Are you counting?"
"No, are you?"

Already seventy-eight.
We'd better quit.

Back to the road the warden pulls up.
He's low key, after all we're after mudders.
We count aloud as we move them
in and out of the bucket water.
Wonder of wonders, seventy-two.
The warden knows the game.
He heads back down river
where the salmon boats land.

We sprinkle cornmeal in the clam water
just as we would steamers.
There'll be a feast
come tomorrow.

Winter

I make these spinners,
small hammered silver blade,
a pink plastic golf tee
and a bead the same color,
a double hook (they don't get hung up
as often as treble hooks)
on stiff wire.

I tie outlandish flies
when I tire of the regulars.
I check the maps
where a wiggling stream
cuts through elevation lines,
my feet getting wet
in daydreams.

Juncos and chickadees visit
as I stare out the window,
the river brown and roiled
waiting for no one.

Steamboat Don

Fishing slowed in winter.
Not that there weren't fish,
but the will to test the cold
against your system diminished.
Winter run steelhead were bigger
than their summer relatives
and fishers built fires on the bank,
plunked roe or lures, then leaned
their rod on a forked stick
while waiting for a strike,
turning back to front and front to back
to keep some survivable temperature.

Don thought trolling was the best way to fish
and one cold January day he invited me
to test his new boat stove.
The firebox stood on wire legs
and took small chunks of wood
with a chimney tall enough
that if you were sitting down,
smoke wouldn't get in the face.
It didn't take away the cold
but you could warm your hands
between checking your line
and running the outboard.

Only once did it become a liability,
when there was a scramble
with a big fish ducking under the boat
and Don moving after it,
me moving at the same time
and the stove keeling over
spreading hot coals on the bottom.

Fire on fiberglass caused a bit of panic
but we had a piss can and a river full of water.

It did look good from a distance,
a run-of-the-mill fourteen footer
chugging along like a steamboat.

Return

Sometimes I forget
in the suffer of day
what the night remembers
running the long beaches
in a rage of freedom.

Moon, still, above the mist,
pulling the endless shadow
from the sea's belly,
are you rock or bone
breathing me back to water?

Spindrift curls in my hand
like a sleeping word.
We press our salted bodies
into the tides of each other
releasing our unutterable selves.

Long Way Home

We took the trail
down a crevice
along the bluff face
to the icy river.
Hours slipped by as we waded,
cold reaching up
cell by cell
toward my heart
as it hammered blood
into numb flesh.
We crisscrossed the stream
a dozen times, wedging
our feet between stones.
Giving in to the current
along sheer rock walls
we aimed at the next
bit of animal trail
or brief respite of beach.
As light faded
we lifted our bodies
to the cabin door.
That night my mouth
would barely open
to accept the soup
a spoon offered.

Crucible

It is that place where we change,
ice to water, wood to flame.

It is swimming into the darkness
and meeting the salamander rising.

It is an open mouth singing.

Nowhere

It's a little bluff overlooking
the river flowing around islands
with willows budded or leafed
or yellow in winter;
the jut of hard rock that water
goes around rather than through,
for now;
the place where an insect floats down
to a waiting trout;
the rounded hills where deer
graze in the evening;
the red splash of poison oak
as hard frost comes;
few people stop
nor should they
there is nothing to sell.

Osprey

Moss soft under my feet
I turn in silence
as the osprey alights
twenty yards away
on a gravel bar
beyond a screen
of vine maple.
It bends to the trout
between its talons
and tears a sun-flash
of flesh away.
It swallows,
reaches for another.

Last Time

He has emphysema and a bad heart valve
the last time we fish the mountain water.
He knows the valve can go anytime,
refuses replacement surgery,
says he's had enough of that.

I take the bridge to the other side
and he slides down the near bank.
Looking into the pool between us
I can see trout hanging in the current.

I watch my father catch a fish
before I get to where the rapids tail out.
It's a big river with fish holding
near the current's edge, behind rocks
and under shadows, waiting for life
to deliver what it will.

It will be several years before
an oxygen tank is necessary
and this communion with the river
is a daydream. So we fish
our separate sides of the same water.

I catch a few small ones
and throw them back. Two keepers
in my creel as I head to our rendezvous.
He makes it up the bank,
stopping now and then to breathe
and I see his four fine rainbows.
He has bragging rights today.

Stone

Like water runs
around the rounding stone
time swims around
the smoothing self
that polished
becomes nothing
but shine.

Cable Crossing

I stop at the cable-crossing hole
when light just touches
the top of the canyon.
I slip down the bank under the trees
to liquid emerald
and roll cast to the rings
of rising trout.
They pay little attention
to my muddler or mayfly.
I set the fly rod down.
This deep green world
turns to magic at twilight
and I give in.
The fish jump and roll
as I breathe the living air.
I will be here at seventeen
and seventy, life washing
through me, this small infinity.

Acknowledgments

These poems originally appeared in, or were accepted at, the following publications, sometimes in an earlier version.

Alexandria Quarterly: "Last Time"
Blue Unicorn: "Osprey"
Canary Literary Journal: "Crucible," "Daybreak, Eagle Rock," "First Cast"
Catamaran Literary Reader: "Wells Creek Run"
Cobra Lily: "After Work," "Lost," "Nowhere"
Eloquent Umbrella: "Return"
Magical Blend: "The Meal"
Manzanita Quarterly: "Stone"
Plum Tree Tavern: "Around the Bend," "Cable Crossing"
Spirit Fish: "Copeland Creek"
Sport Literate: "In Stream," "Phantom"
Stonecrop Magazine: "Monsters All"
Turtle Island Quarterly: "River Bend"
Valley View News: "Rock Creek Camp"
Windfall: "Brockton Store," "Clams"

"Copeland Creek," "The Meal," and "Stone" were included in the chapbook *Tasting the River in the Salmon's Flesh*, Traprock Books.

Thank you to Vince Wixon and Dorothy Swain for help with this manuscript.

About the Author

A lifelong Oregonian, Gary Lark has been a carpenter, janitor, hospital aide, salesman, storyteller, fly fisherman and librarian. His work includes *Ordinary Gravity*, Airlie Press; *River of Solace*, winner of the Editor's Choice Chapbook Award from Turtle Island Quarterly, Flowstone Press; *In the House of Memory*, BatCat Press; *Without a Map*, Wellstone Press; and *Getting By*, winner of the Holland Prize. He and his wife Dorothy live in the Rogue Valley.